STOP OVER THINKING:

GO OUT AND COME IN WITH NEW IDEAS

BY

MATTHEW RICHES

TABLE OF CONTENTS

INTRODUCTION

In the beginning:

In the fast-paced and demanding world we occupy, the phenomenon of overthinking has become increasingly prominent, affecting individuals across all backgrounds and circumstances. Overthinking, characterized by frequent and intrusive thoughts that lead to excessive concern and rumination, can weaken mental well-being and affect productivity, relationships, and the general quality of life. From the banal issues of daily life to the weightier matters of professional choices and personal relationships, overthinking can penetrate every part of our lives, leaving us immobilized by indecision and tormented by doubt. Understanding the complexities of overthinking, its underlying causes, and its far-reaching implications is vital for managing the challenges of modern life and building a healthier relationship with our thoughts and emotions. In this research, we delve into the depths of overthinking, analyzing its psychological mechanisms, societal repercussions, and solutions for prevention and treatment. Through insight and introspection, we strive to understand the complexities of overthinking and illuminate avenues to greater clarity, resilience, and peace of mind.

In the frenetic speed of contemporary life, stress has developed as a widespread force, impacting individuals, communities, and cultures globally. From the responsibilities of work and education to the complexities of personal relationships and societal obligations, the sensation of stress is an essential component of the human condition. Defined as the body's physiological and psychological response to perceived threats or challenges, stress can emerge in numerous forms, ranging from moderate agitation to chronic worry. While some degree of stress is a natural and adaptive response to life's exigencies, persistent or excessive stress can exact a heavy toll on mental and physical well-being, leading to a multitude of unfavorable health effects and lowering the overall quality of life. Understanding the multidimensional nature of stress, its underlying mechanisms, and its influence on individual and collective health is crucial to managing this pervasive phenomenon and fostering resilience in the face of adversity. In this research, we go on a quest to unravel the complexity of stress, diving into its origins, manifestations, and implications for human flourishing. Through a comprehensive investigation of stress and its numerous dimensions, we attempt to highlight routes to increased well-being, balance, and resilience in an increasingly stress-laden society.

FIRST CHAPTER
WHAT IS YOUR APPROACH TO UNDERSTANDING STRATEGY?

Overthinking is a cognitive process in which an individual unduly focuses on ideas, anxieties, or considerations linked to a certain circumstance, problem, or decision. The phrase "overthinking" refers to this cognitive activity. To put it simply, it is the act of thinking excessively or spending an excessive amount of time analyzing, dissecting, and brooding over numerous elements of a specific subject.

Overthinking is characterized by the individual's tendency to continually replay scenarios in their mind, examine a large number of alternatives and potential consequences, and scrutinize minutiae to such an extent that it becomes unproductive. It is common for individuals to have feelings of stress, worry, and hesitation as a result of excessive thinking. This is because the individual may have difficulty finding closure or making a clear decision amidst the multitude of thoughts and concerns.

There are many different situations in which one could find themselves engaging in excessive thinking, such as personal relationships, work-related issues, academic endeavors, and everyday life events. An excessive inclination to focus excessively on present situations, excessively worry about future outcomes, or excessively reflect on events that have occurred in the past is a defining characteristic of this condition.

Overthinking becomes troublesome when it interferes with one's capacity to work efficiently or have a sense of serenity and well-being. While some reflection and analysis can be helpful in the process of problem-solving and decision-making, overthinking becomes extremely problematic when it interferes with these abilities. Individuals can cultivate more mental clarity, reduce stress levels, and make decisions with more confidence if they learn to recognize and regulate their tendency to engage in excessive thinking. Overthinking is a cognitive process characterized by extensive and often needless rumination, analysis, and deliberation of a situation, problem, or conclusion. It entails ruminating on thoughts, options, and potential outcomes to the extent that it becomes unproductive and may lead to greater tension, anxiety, and indecision.

Here are some of the key components of overthinking:

1. **Repetitive Thoughts**: Overthinkers tend to replay circumstances or ideas constantly in their minds, frequently without making progress towards a resolution.

2. **Analysis Paralysis**: Overthinking can lead to a state of analysis paralysis, where individuals become so consumed with weighing choices and potential repercussions that they fail to make decisions or take action.

3. **Magnification of Problems**: Overthinkers may blow modest concerns out of proportion, giving disproportionate emphasis to trivial facts or potential outcomes.

4. **Fear of Making Mistakes**: Overthinking is typically fuelled by a fear of making the incorrect decision or adopting the wrong course of action, forcing individuals to engage in endless mental acrobatics to prevent perceived blunders.

5. Difficulty in Letting Go: Overthinkers may find it tough to let go of thoughts or concerns, even when they are irrelevant or beyond their control.

6. **Negative Self-Talk**: Overthinking is typically accompanied by negative self-talk, self-doubt, and a tendency to linger on past mistakes or faults.

7. **Impact on Well-Being**: Overthinking can have adverse impacts on mental and emotional well-being, contributing to stress, anxiety, insomnia, and even depression in severe situations.

Addressing overthinking often entails adopting skills to handle intrusive thoughts and promote mindfulness, such as:

practicing mindfulness and grounding practices to stay present and focused on the current moment.
setting restrictions on the amount of time spent analyzing a topic or decision.
challenging illogical or excessive thoughts through cognitive restructuring.
engaging in relaxation methods, such as deep breathing or meditation, to reduce

stress and increase mental clarity.
Seeking support from friends, family, or
mental health specialists to gain perspective
and create coping methods.

By identifying the signs and effects of
overthinking and practicing healthy coping
methods, individuals can learn to manage
their thoughts more efficiently and make
decisions with better confidence and clarity.

CHAPTER TWO

WHAT BRINGS ABOUT OVERTHINKING

Overthinking can come from several underlying reasons, including psychological, cognitive, and environmental issues. Here are some common causes of overthinking:

1. **Perfectionism**: People who strive for perfection may find themselves overthinking things because they fear making mistakes or not matching their high expectations. They may constantly evaluate details and options to ensure everything aligns precisely.

2. **Anxiety and Stress**: Anxiety and stress can promote overthinking as individuals obsess over prospective threats, undesirable consequences, or worst-case scenarios. The dread of failure or uncertainty can prolong a cycle of overthinking, leading to increased anxiety.

3. **Poor self-esteem**: Individuals with poor self-esteem may continually second-guess themselves and worry about how others see them. They may overthink social situations, seeing innocent statements or behaviors as criticism or rejection.

4. **Past Trauma or Unfavorable Experiences**: Previous traumatic experiences or unpleasant occurrences can lead to overthinking as individuals try to make sense of what happened, foresee similar situations, or avoid future harm. They may relive past incidents in their brains, seeking to discover reasons or strategies to avert such occurrences.

5. **Lack of confidence**: People who lack confidence in their abilities or judgment may overthink decisions and behaviors, seeking reassurance or approval from others. They may hesitate to trust their instincts and continuously seek external approval, leading to hesitation and overanalysis.

6. **High Sensitivity**: Highly sensitive people may be more prone to overthinking due to their heightened awareness of subtleties and nuances in their environment. They may overanalyze social signs, environmental stimuli, and human relationships, which can be emotionally taxing.

7. **Rumination**: Rumination entails repetitively concentrating on bad ideas, feelings, or experiences without finding a resolution. It can be a symptom of depression or other mood disorders and can contribute to overthinking as individuals seek to break free from unpleasant thought patterns.

8. **Cognitive Biases**: Cognitive biases, such as confirmation bias or catastrophizing, can lead to overthinking by distorting perceptions and altering how individuals understand information. They may selectively focus on evidence that validates

their previous beliefs or amplifies the severity of perceived threats or risks.

9. **Overloaded Schedule**: A busy or chaotic lifestyle with various duties and commitments can overwhelm individuals, leading to overthinking as they try to juggle multiple chores and priorities. They may worry about forgetting something crucial or failing to fulfill deadlines, leading to excessive mental rumination.

10. **Lack of problem-solving abilities**: Individuals who lack good problem-solving abilities may resort to overthinking as a coping mechanism when presented with obstacles or uncertainty. They may struggle to identify viable alternatives or make decisions, leading to protracted periods of analysis and indecision.

Addressing the underlying reasons for overthinking often entails gaining self-awareness, practicing mindfulness, getting assistance from others, and adopting healthy coping mechanisms to handle stress, anxiety, and negative thought patterns.

How do repetitive thoughts bring about overthinking?

Repetitive thoughts play a crucial role in the development and persistence of overthinking. Here's how:

1. **Increased Focus**: Repetitive ideas often become the focal object of one's attention. When a certain thought or concern recurs repeatedly, it holds the individual's mental focus, making it difficult to transfer attention elsewhere.

2. **Amplification of Importance**: With each repetition, the relevance of the notion may be increased in the individual's mind. The more an idea recurs, the more weight and

importance it may seem to hold, even if it is objectively insignificant.

3. **Rumination**: Repetitive ideas often lead to rumination, which entails continuously ruminating on the same thoughts, feelings, or issues. Rumination can heighten negative emotions, such as anxiety or grief, and prolong their length, adding to a cycle of overthinking.

4. **Inability to Let Go**: Repetitive thoughts can make it tough for folks to let go of a particular concern or notion. Even when they try to distract themselves or focus on other issues, the continual recurrence of the thought keeps them from totally disengaging from it.

5. **Interference with Problem-Solving**: While some level of introspection and analysis is important for problem-solving, recurrent ideas might hamper the process. Instead of enabling clarity and insight, the

frequent repetition of the same thoughts may lead to mental stagnation and indecision.

6. **Negative Feedback Loop**: Repetitive thoughts often generate a negative feedback loop when the more a person thinks about a certain topic, the more entrenched and overwhelming it gets. This loop maintains the cycle of overthinking and makes it increasingly difficult to break out of repetitive mental patterns.

7. **Impact on Emotional Well-Being**: The persistence of recurrent thoughts can take a toll on an individual's emotional well-being. It can add to emotions of tension, worry, and frustration as individuals seek relief from the persistent mental chatter.

To address the impact of recurring ideas on overthinking, individuals might apply measures such as mindfulness techniques, cognitive restructuring, and distraction methods. These approaches can help individuals gain perspective, confront unhelpful thought patterns, and establish healthier ways of managing their mental processes. Additionally, seeking support from mental health specialists or engaging in therapy can provide essential tools and insights for managing recurrent thoughts and lowering overthinking tendencies.

How Does Lack of Confidence Bring About Overthinking?

Lack of confidence can considerably contribute to overthinking by diminishing a person's belief in their abilities, judgments, and conclusions. Here's how it brings about overthinking, along with examples:

1. **Second-Guessing Decisions**: When individuals lack confidence in their decision-making ability, they typically second-guess themselves. They may continuously scrutinize their choices,

seeking comfort or affirmation from others, which can lead to overthinking. For example, someone who lacks confidence can spend an excessive amount of time agonizing over which employment offer to take, worried they will make the incorrect decision and regret it later.

2. **Dread of Failure**: A lack of confidence might exacerbate the dread of failure. Individuals may overthink potential outcomes, focusing on the negative ramifications of their actions rather than recognizing the possibility of success. For instance, a student who lacks confidence in their academic abilities would overanalyze every test question, thinking they would earn a bad score and disappoint themselves or others.

3. **Seeking External Validation**: People who lack confidence frequently rely significantly on external validation to reinforce their worth and actions. They may

continually seek acceptance from others, leading to overthinking as they strive to predict and meet others' expectations. For example, someone with poor self-esteem can overthink their wardrobe choice for a social occasion, fretting about whether others will approve of their appearance.

4. **Difficulty with assertiveness**: A lack of confidence can hamper assertiveness and self-expression. Individuals may hesitate to share their thoughts or establish their needs, fearing rejection or criticism. This hesitancy might lead to overthinking as they fret over the potential consequences of speaking up. For instance, an employee who lacks confidence in their ideas can overthink whether to share their proposals during a team meeting, wondering about how they will be received by colleagues and superiors.

5. **Comparing Oneself to Others**: Individuals with low confidence typically engage in negative self-comparisons,

measuring themselves against others and focusing on perceived faults. This constant comparison can foster feelings of inadequacy and deepen overthinking as individuals seek to reach unattainable standards. For example, someone who lacks confidence in their appearance could overthink social encounters, continually comparing themselves to others and worrying about being assessed for their perceived defects.

Addressing the core causes of poor confidence, such as negative self-talk, past experiences of failure or rejection, and excessive expectations, might help individuals moderate overthinking tendencies. Building self-esteem, practicing self-compassion, and confronting negative ideas can allow individuals to trust their intuition, make decisions with greater confidence, and reduce overthinking in numerous aspects of their lives.

DOES OVERTHINKING EXIST?

Yes, overthinking does exist as a recognized cognitive condition experienced by many individuals. Overthinking refers to a pattern of excessive rumination, analysis, and pondering of thoughts, ideas, or circumstances beyond what is necessary or productive.

Here's why overthinking exists:

1. **Complexity of Human Thought**: The human mind is sophisticated and multifaceted, capable of digesting large amounts of information and generating varied thoughts and interpretations. However, this intricacy can occasionally lead to overthinking, where individuals become locked in cycles of repeated or unproductive thinking habits.

2. **Anxiety and Stress**: Anxiety and stress are major factors in overthinking. When individuals are overwhelmed by uncertainty, worry, or pressure, they may engage in excessive analysis and rumination as a coping mechanism. This heightened state of arousal can intensify cognitive processes, making it difficult for individuals to disengage from recurrent ideas.

3. **Cognitive Biases**: Cognitive biases, such as confirmation bias or catastrophizing, can lead to overthinking by distorting perceptions and altering how individuals understand information. These biases may cause individuals to selectively focus on bad consequences or exaggerated possibilities, exacerbating the tendency to overanalyze.

4. **Perfectionism and Fear of Failure**: Perfectionism, or the pursuit of flawlessness, can push individuals to overthink as they seek to satisfy impossible standards or avoid making mistakes. The fear of failure can

intensify this tendency, forcing individuals to engage in intensive mental processing to prevent perceived errors or weaknesses.

5. **Rumination and Emotional Regulation**: Rumination, the repetitive focus on negative thoughts or feelings, is closely linked to overthinking. Individuals may ruminate as a strategy to cope with upsetting experiences or unsolved concerns, but this process generally leads to heightened anxiety and prolonged states of rumination.

6. **Lack of Confidence and Decision-Making Difficulty**: Individuals who lack confidence in their abilities or struggle with decision-making may overthink options and scenarios in an attempt to avoid making mistakes. This ambiguity and self-doubt can create a cycle of hesitation and overanalysis, making it challenging for individuals to trust their intuition or make clear decisions.

Overall, overthinking can have severe impacts on mental well-being, leading to increased tension, worry, and indecision. While some level of thought and analysis is needed for problem-solving and self-reflection, excessive rumination can interfere with productivity, emotional control, and the general quality of life. Recognizing the signs and triggers of overthinking and implementing healthy coping methods can help individuals control their thought processes more efficiently and nurture greater mental clarity and resilience.

CHAPTER THREE

CONSEQUENCES OF OVERTHINKING

Overthinking can have many implications, impacting people both psychologically and emotionally. Here are some common consequences of overthinking, along with examples:

1. **Increased Stress and Anxiety**: Overthinking sometimes leads to heightened stress and anxiety levels when individuals repeatedly concentrate on prospective difficulties, uncertainties, or undesirable outcomes. For example, someone could overthink a social gathering, worrying about how others perceive them and anticipating numerous embarrassing circumstances.

2. **Impaired Decision-Making**:
Overthinking might interfere with the
capacity to make judgments confidently and
efficiently. Individuals may become stuck
by indecision, endlessly evaluating the
advantages and cons without resolving. For
instance, a person could overthink career
possibilities to the extent of missing
application deadlines or prospects.

3. **Poor Sleep Quality**: Overthinking can
interrupt sleep patterns, leading to insomnia
or restless nights. Individuals may struggle
to calm their brains, reliving problems and
scenarios when they should be relaxing. For
example, someone can overthink a quarrel
with a friend, making it difficult to unwind
and go to sleep.

4. **Negative Impact on Relationships**:
Overthinking can strain relationships by
causing individuals to perceive others'
behavior adversely or by creating unneeded
confrontations. For instance, a person could

overthink a friend's delayed response to a message, assuming it represents a change in the relationship dynamics and resulting in unneeded stress.

5. **Reduced Productivity**: Excessive rumination can divert attention and energy away from tasks, limiting overall productivity. Individuals may find it tough to focus on their tasks owing to continuous thoughts about extraneous subjects. For example, an employee could overthink a little mistake made earlier in the day, affecting their ability to concentrate on their current tasks.

6. **Physical Health Impacts**: Chronic overthinking can contribute to physical health issues such as headaches, muscle tension, and gastrointestinal disorders. The mind-body connection means that chronic mental stress can emerge physically. For example, someone who overthinks money

matters could develop stomachaches or tension headaches.

7. **Impact on Mood and Well-Being**: Overthinking is generally related to negative thought patterns, leading to feelings of melancholy, irritation, or hopelessness. For instance, an individual could overthink prior failures, contributing to a chronic bad mood and lower overall well-being.

8. **Worsening of Mental Health Issues**: Overthinking can exacerbate existing mental health issues, such as depression or generalized anxiety disorder. For example, someone with anxiety may overthink social encounters, heightening emotions of dread and self-doubt.

9. **Strained Creativity**: Overthinking can impede creative processes by restricting spontaneous ideas and free thinking. A person may become so consumed with

evaluating prospective consequences that they fail to produce fresh solutions or ideas.

10. **Isolation and Withdrawal**: Persistent overthinking may lead individuals to withdraw from social activities, fearing the mental burden involved with social connections. For example, someone can avoid social activities owing to overthinking potentially unpleasant times or fearing judgment from others.

Addressing overthinking frequently entails increasing awareness, finding assistance from others, and adopting healthy coping techniques to manage stress and anxiety. Professional guidance, such as therapy, can be beneficial in helping individuals stop the cycle of overthinking and create more adaptive thought habits.

PROCRASTINATION AND OVERDEPENDENCE

Procrastination and overdependency can indeed lead to tension and disappointment due to several reasons:

1. **Procrastination**:
Increased pressure: Procrastination often results in postponed work and deadlines. As deadlines approach, individuals may experience heightened stress owing to the pressure of completing activities within a restricted timeframe.

Reduced Quality of Work: Rushing to accomplish activities at the last minute can damage the quality of work. Individuals may feel disappointed with their performance or outcomes, resulting in a cycle of tension and discontent.

Loss of Control: Procrastination can make individuals feel as though they have lost control of their duties and time management. This sensation of lack of control can add to emotions of tension and worry.

Negative Impact on Self-Esteem: Chronic procrastination can damage self-esteem and confidence. Individuals may feel dissatisfied with themselves for not reaching their standards, resulting in greater stress and self-criticism.

2. **Over-Dependency**:

loss of autonomy: over-dependency on others can lead to a loss of autonomy and self-reliance. Individuals may feel overwhelmed and frustrated when they continually rely on others to make decisions or handle problems for them.

Fear of Abandonment or Rejection: Over-dependent individuals may fear being abandoned or rejected if they do not receive the help they expect from others. This anxiety can lead to tension and disappointment when others are unavailable or unable to meet their requirements.

Disappointment in Others: Over-dependent individuals may feel disappointed when others fail to match their expectations or provide the level of support they desire. This can lead to strained relationships and feelings of animosity.

Limited Personal Growth: Overdependency can hamper personal growth and development. Individuals may feel disappointed in themselves for not taking the initiative or being able to tackle issues autonomously. This might add to feelings of tension and unhappiness with one's life situation.

In summary, both procrastination and overdependency can produce stress and disappointment by diminishing individual productivity, autonomy, and self-esteem. Overcoming these behaviors includes adopting healthy coping techniques, increasing time management skills, building self-reliance, and creating boundaries in relationships. By addressing these behaviors, individuals can reduce stress and disappointment and increase their general well-being and pleasure in life.

OVERSPENDING AND LUXURY LIFESTYLE

Overspending and sustaining a luxury lifestyle can undoubtedly contribute to depression, although it's important to note that depression can emerge from a variety of variables and is often impacted by individual circumstances and predispositions. Here's how expenditures and a fancy lifestyle might potentially lead to depression:

1. **Financial Stress**: Overspending typically leads to financial pressure and debt. Constantly living beyond one's means can generate a tremendous financial burden, generating worry, anxiety, and feelings of helplessness. The pressure to maintain a

specific lifestyle despite financial challenges might increase these negative emotions and contribute to sadness.

2. **Insecurity and Comparison**: Maintaining a luxury lifestyle may be influenced by cultural pressures and a desire to fit in or appear successful. Constantly comparing oneself to others who appear to have more wealth or things can lead to feelings of inadequacy and low self-esteem. This can contribute to depression since individuals may feel they are not living up to societal expectations or their ideals.

3. **Emotional emptiness**: Some people may utilize material belongings and luxury goods as a means of filling an emotional emptiness or seeking validation. However, the satisfaction received from worldly items is typically transient and superficial. Over time, individuals may realize that worldly wealth does not give permanent satisfaction

or fulfillment, leading to a sense of emptiness and sadness.

4. **Relationship Strain**: Overspending and sustaining a luxurious lifestyle can strain relationships with loved ones, particularly if financial decisions are made without joint agreement or concern for others' needs. Conflicts about money can produce stress, resentment, and feelings of isolation, which can contribute to depression.

5. **Financial effects**: Overspending can have major long-term financial effects, such as bankruptcy, foreclosure, or loss of assets. Facing these financial challenges can be emotionally distressing and lead to feelings of hopelessness, despair, and melancholy.

6. **Identity Crisis**: Relying largely on material items and a luxury lifestyle for self-worth and identity can lead to an identity crisis when external causes, such as financial setbacks or changes in

circumstances, disturb this lifestyle. Individuals may struggle to reframe their sense of self and purpose, resulting in feelings of bewilderment and sadness.

It's crucial for those who are suffering from depression or associated symptoms to get support from mental health specialists. Therapy, counseling, and support groups can provide helpful tools and strategies for managing depression, resolving underlying difficulties, and boosting general well-being. Additionally, adopting healthy attitudes towards money and material possessions, practicing mindfulness, and focusing on meaningful connections and experiences can help individuals cultivate greater pleasure and fulfillment in life.

CHAPTER FOUR

HOW TO DO AWAY WITH OVERTHINKING AND STRESS

Managing overthinking and stress entails adopting healthy coping methods and establishing resilience to navigate life's obstacles efficiently. Here are some strategies to help decrease overthinking and stress:

1. **Practice mindfulness**: Mindfulness exercises, such as deep breathing, meditation, and body scans, can help anchor your consciousness in the present moment. Mindfulness facilitates the acceptance of thoughts and emotions without judgment, which helps lessen overthinking and stress.

2. **Set Boundaries**: Establish clear boundaries to safeguard your time, energy, and emotional well-being. Learn to say no to excessive commitments and prioritize

activities that correspond with your values and ambitions.

3. **Question Negative Thoughts**: Practice cognitive restructuring to question negative thought patterns and replace them with more realistic and optimistic viewpoints. Question the veracity of your views and consider other interpretations of situations.

4. **Focus on answers**: Instead of obsessing about difficulties, focus on identifying realistic answers and making aggressive efforts to address challenges. Break projects into reasonable increments and reward achievement, no matter how tiny.

5. **Engage in Physical Activity**: Regular exercise is a potent stress reliever and mood enhancer. Engage in activities you enjoy, such as walking, jogging, yoga, or dancing, to release tension and raise endorphins.

6. **Maintain a Healthy Lifestyle**: Prioritize self-care activities, including nutritious

meals, appropriate sleep, and relaxing techniques. Avoid excessive caffeine, alcohol, and stimulants, as these might worsen stress and anxiety.

7. **Practice Time Management**: Use time management practices, such as prioritizing activities, developing timetables, and setting deadlines, to boost productivity and eliminate procrastination. Break projects into smaller tasks and provide specific time blocks for focused work.

8. **Seek social support**: Connect with sympathetic friends, family members, or support groups to discuss your ideas and experiences. Social support can provide perspective, validation, and encouragement during hard circumstances.

9. **Limit Media Consumption**: Limit exposure to unfavorable news and social media, which can drive worry and overthinking. Choose credible sources of

information and take pauses from screens to focus on activities that promote relaxation and enjoyment.

10. **Seek expert help**: If overthinking and stress persist despite your efforts to handle them, consider obtaining help from a mental health expert. Therapy, counseling, or cognitive-behavioral approaches can provide tailored solutions for coping with stress and enhancing general well-being.

By adopting these tactics into your daily routine and prioritizing self-care, you may create resilience, eliminate overthinking, and better handle stress in your life. Remember that development takes time and patience, so be gentle with yourself as you navigate your journey toward more balance and peace of mind.

RELATIONSHIPS AND DRUG ABUSE

Relationship troubles and drug usage can contribute to overthinking in numerous ways, increasing mental health challenges and sustaining negative thought patterns. Here's how each of these variables might contribute to overthinking:

1. **Relationship Issues**:

a. **communicating problems**: Difficulties in communicating within relationships can lead to misunderstandings, unresolved disputes, and unexpressed emotions. Individuals may overthink interactions and conversations, trying to interpret hidden meanings or anticipate replies from their partner.

b. Insecurity and Jealousy: Insecure attachment patterns and feelings of jealousy can encourage overthinking in partnerships. Individuals may excessively examine their partner's actions, seeking reassurance or confirmation to assuage their concerns.

c. Fear of Rejection or Abandonment: Past experiences of rejection or abandonment might generate fears of intimacy and vulnerability in relationships. Individuals may overthink their worth of love and validation, continually seeking indications of reassurance from their relationship.

d. Idealization and Disappointment: Unrealistic expectations and idealization of partners can lead to disappointment and disillusionment in relationships. Individuals may overthink perceived defects or differences between their desired picture and reality, leading to feelings of dissatisfaction and uneasiness.

e. Lack of Trust: Trust concerns can erode the foundation of relationships, leading to mistrust, uncertainty, and overthinking.

Individuals may constantly examine their partner's actions and intentions, fearing betrayal or dishonesty.

2. **Drug Abuse**:

a. **Escapism and Avoidance**: Drug usage can act as a type of escapism from underlying emotional anguish, stress, or relationship problems. Individuals may use drugs to dull uncomfortable feelings or temporarily divert themselves from overthinking and unfavorable thought patterns.

b. **Impaired Cognitive Functioning**: Substance misuse can affect cognitive functioning and decision-making abilities, leaving individuals more susceptible to overthinking and irrational thought patterns. Drug-induced paranoia and anxiety may aggravate overthinking and contribute to heightened stress levels.

c. Cycle of reliance: Substance abuse can sustain a cycle of reliance and negative reinforcement. Individuals may become locked into a routine of utilizing drugs to cope with overthinking and stress, leading to increased tolerance, withdrawal symptoms, and cravings.

d. Relationship Strain: Drug misuse can strain relationships and destroy trust and communication between partners. Individuals may overthink the consequences of their substance usage on their relationships, resulting in feelings of guilt, humiliation, and solitude.

e. Co-occurring Mental Health Issues: Substance abuse typically co-occurs with mental health illnesses, such as anxiety, depression, and trauma-related disorders. These underlying difficulties might contribute to overthinking and increase the negative implications of substance usage on relationships and overall well-being.

In summary, relationship troubles and substance usage can worsen overthinking by fueling insecurities, prompting phobias, decreasing cognitive functioning, and compromising emotional well-being. Seeking treatment from mental health specialists, participating in healthy coping methods, and cultivating open communication within relationships are critical steps in treating overthinking and maintaining overall mental health and relational well-being.

SELF-ISOLATION AND GENDER DISCRIMINATION

Self-isolation and gender discrimination can indeed contribute to overthinking by intensifying feelings of loneliness, social exclusion, and unfairness. Here's how each of these variables might contribute to overthinking:

1. Self-Isolation:

a. **Lack of Social Connection**: Self-isolation frequently implies a lack of social engagement and support networks. Individuals who self-isolate may feel alienated from others, resulting in feelings of loneliness and isolation. Without social connection, individuals may spend more time ruminating on their ideas and feelings, which can contribute to overthinking.

b. **Rumination and Negative Thought Patterns**: In the absence of external diversions and social activities, individuals in self-isolation may indulge in excessive rumination and negative thought patterns. Without external stimuli to occupy their minds, they may dwell on fears, anxieties, and prior experiences, leading to overthinking and heightened stress levels.

c. Limited Perspective and Input: Self-isolation can limit individuals' exposure to varied perspectives and input from others. Without external information and validation, individuals may rely only on their thoughts and perceptions, which can worsen overthinking and distort their view of reality.

d. Emotional discomfort and uncertainty: Self-isolation can worsen emotions of emotional discomfort and uncertainty, particularly during tough times or crises. Individuals may feel overwhelmed by unpleasant feelings and uncertainties about the future, resulting in excessive rumination and overthinking as they seek to cope with their situation.

2. Gender Discrimination:

a. Internalization of preconceptions: Gender discrimination can drive individuals to internalize unfavorable preconceptions and biases about themselves and others. Women, for example, may internalize cultural messages about their perceived inferiority or limits, leading to feelings of self-doubt and inadequacy. These ingrained ideas might contribute to overthinking as individuals constantly doubt their worth and ability.

b. Imposter Syndrome: Gender discrimination can fuel imposter syndrome, a psychological disorder where individuals doubt their successes and fear being discovered as false. Women and underrepresented genders may suffer from imposter syndrome more frequently due to cultural expectations and biases. This persistent worry of being "found out" can lead to overthinking and self-sabotage as individuals second-guess their abilities and successes.

c. Microaggressions and Gaslighting: Gender discrimination typically emerges as microaggressions, subtle forms of discrimination, or invalidation based on gender. Women and marginalized genders may undergo gaslighting, where their feelings and views are disregarded or invalidated. These events can lead to overthinking as individuals question their reality and internalize sentiments of self-doubt and worthlessness.

d. Unequal Opportunities and Resources: Gender discrimination can limit access to opportunities, resources, and support networks for women and marginalized genders. This imbalance can contribute to feelings of irritation, powerlessness, and unfairness, leading to overthinking as individuals manage structural barriers and societal expectations.

In summary, self-isolation and gender discrimination can worsen overthinking by intensifying emotions of loneliness, social exclusion, internalized biases, and structural injustices. It's crucial for people experiencing these challenges to seek help from mental health specialists, participate in self-care activities, and advocate for systemic change to address underlying issues and promote mental well-being.

EXERCISE AND GOOD INTERPERSONAL FRIENDSHIP

Exercise and excellent interpersonal interactions can be significant aids for minimizing overthinking and boosting mental well-being in various ways.

1. **Exercise:**

a. Stress Reduction: Physical activity, such as exercise, has been demonstrated to reduce levels of stress hormones like cortisol and adrenaline in the body. Regular exercise helps to release tension and promote relaxation, making it simpler to manage stress and anxiety that lead to overthinking.

b. Mood Enhancement: Exercise boosts the production of endorphins, neurotransmitters that function as natural mood lifters. Engaging in regular physical activity can improve mood and overall psychological well-being, reducing the frequency and severity of negative thoughts linked with overthinking.

c. Distraction and Focus: Exercise provides a healthy distraction from rumination and overthinking by diverting attention to the current moment and physical sensations. Focusing on the movements of the body during exercise can help individuals break free from recurrent thought patterns and acquire mental clarity.

d. Improved Sleep Quality: Regular exercise has been related to improved sleep quality and duration. Adequate sleep is critical for cognitive performance and emotional control, helping individuals better cope with stress and manage overthinking during waking hours.

e. Sense of Achievement: Setting and attaining fitness goals through exercise can enhance self-esteem and confidence. Accomplishing milestones, whether it's completing a hard workout or reaching a new fitness level, promotes a sense of competence and mastery, minimizing feelings of self-doubt and rumination.

2. **Good interpersonal friendships**:

a. **Social Support**: Positive social ties provide emotional support and affirmation, buffering against the negative consequences of stress and overthinking. Having friends who listen non-judgmentally, offer support, and provide perspective can help people feel understood and appreciated.

b. **Validation and Perspective**: Interpersonal friendships allow validation and perspective-taking. Friends can offer different ideas, question unreasonable notions, and provide reassurance during moments of doubt, helping individuals acquire clarity and confidence in their decision-making.

c. **Shared Activities and Distraction**: Engaging in shared activities with friends can serve as a good distraction from overthinking. Participating in enjoyable social activities, such as hobbies, sports, or outings, allows individuals to focus on the present moment and interact with others, reducing rumination and stress.

d. **Emotional Regulation**: Good friendships foster emotional regulation and resilience by offering avenues for the expression and processing of feelings. Sharing ideas and feelings with trustworthy companions can help individuals control intense emotions, manage stress, and gain perspective on hard situations.

e. **Sense of Belonging**: Interpersonal friendships fulfill the innate human urge for belonging and connection. Feeling linked to a supportive social network lowers feelings of isolation and loneliness, which are major triggers for overthinking and mental anguish.

In summary, exercise and excellent interpersonal interactions serve complementary functions in minimizing overthinking and enhancing mental well-being. By including regular physical activity in their routine and developing strong social connections, individuals can cultivate resilience, handle stress, and develop healthier mental patterns.

RELIGIOUS CONTRIBUTION AND FAMILY SUPPORT

Religious contributions and family support can play crucial roles in either alleviating or worsening overthinking, depending on individual experiences and belief systems. Here's how each aspect may affect overthinking:

1. **Religious Contributions**:

a. **Belief Systems**: Religious beliefs and practices can alter individuals' perceptions of the world and provide frameworks for comprehending life's obstacles and uncertainties. For some individuals, religious teachings may bring peace, comfort, and a sense of purpose, decreasing the need for excessive rumination and overthinking about existential concerns.

b. Coping methods: Religious practices, such as prayer, meditation, and seeking spiritual guidance, can serve as coping methods during times of stress and uncertainty. Engaging in religious rituals and connecting with a higher power may offer individuals a sense of control, perspective, and hope, helping to alleviate overthinking and worry.

c. Community Support: Religious communities frequently create social support networks where individuals can find belonging, acceptance, and understanding. Participating in religious gatherings, support groups, and community service activities can establish connections and relationships that buffer against feelings of isolation and loneliness, common triggers for overthinking.

d. Interpretation of Religious Doctrine: While religious teachings can bring comfort and guidance, they may also contribute to overthinking if understood in strict or dogmatic ways. Individuals who suffer from questions, conflicts, or guilt connected to religious beliefs may engage in excessive rumination and self-criticism, leading to heightened anxiety and distress.

2. **Family Support**:

a. **Emotional Validation**: Family support gives emotional validation and acceptance, which are vital for boosting mental well-being and minimizing overthinking. Open communication, empathy, and affirmation from family members can help individuals feel understood, appreciated, and supported in times of stress and uncertainty.

b. Problem-Solving Assistance: Families can serve as helpful resources for problem-solving and coping with life's obstacles. Supportive family members offer practical guidance, perspective, and encouragement, helping individuals handle challenging situations and make educated decisions, eliminating the need for excessive rumination and overthinking.

c. Role Modeling: Family dynamics and relationships can impact individuals' attitudes and habits towards overthinking. Positive role modeling of healthy coping methods, effective communication, and perseverance in the face of adversity can enable individuals to manage stress and uncertainty more successfully, lowering the inclination to overthink.

d. Interpersonal Conflict: While family support can be useful, dysfunctional family dynamics or interpersonal conflict may add to overthinking and stress. Conflicts, unresolved conflicts, and a lack of communication within families can produce emotional turbulence and anxiety, prompting individuals to ruminate excessively about their relationships and surroundings.

In summary, religious contributions and family support can play intricate roles in shaping individuals' experiences of overthinking. While they can provide comfort, direction, and social support that alleviate overthinking, they may also add stress and uncertainty if experienced in bad or contradictory ways. Cultivating strong connections, establishing open communication, and seeking support from religious or familial networks can help individuals overcome problems and enhance their mental well-being.

CHAPTER FIVE

CONCLUSION

In conclusion, the influence of overthinking and stress extends beyond the individual level, affecting families, communities, and societies as a whole. Overthinking, defined by excessive rumination and worry, can lead to heightened stress levels and bad emotional outcomes for individuals, with far-reaching repercussions for broader social systems.

At the individual level, overthinking can impair decision-making, alter sleep habits, and lead to mental health illnesses such as anxiety and depression. Persistent stress stemming from overthinking can affect physical health, weaken immunological function, and diminish the overall quality of life for individuals.

Within families, overthinking and stress can strain relationships, damage trust, and create communication hurdles. Family members may feel heightened tension and conflict as a result of unique pressures and coping processes. In turn, family interactions can worsen or reduce stress levels, altering individuals' skills to cope with overthinking and its accompanying issues.

In communities, the cumulative effects of pervasive overthinking and stress can manifest in social isolation, lower productivity, and compromised well-being. Community support networks and resources play a significant role in minimizing the harmful effects of stress by creating relationships, promoting resilience, and giving access to mental health services and assistance.

At the national level, the frequency of overthinking and stress can have substantial economic and societal effects. High levels of stress relate to healthcare costs, absenteeism, and reduced productivity in the workforce. Moreover, systemic factors such as discrimination, socioeconomic inequality, and political turmoil can aggravate stress levels within communities and throughout the nation.

Addressing overthinking and stress involves a holistic strategy that encompasses individual self-care practices, supportive family and community contexts, and systemic interventions targeted at boosting mental health and resilience. Education, awareness campaigns, and legislative measures can help destigmatize mental health disorders, expand access to resources, and build supportive environments that value holistic well-being for people, families, communities, and the nation as a whole. By acknowledging the interconnectivity of overthinking and stress across many levels of society, we can strive towards establishing healthier, more resilient communities that emphasize mental health and communal well-being.

MOTIVATIONAL SPEECH AND GOOD MUSIC

Motivational speeches and good music can play key roles in minimizing overthinking by altering mood, mindset, and emotional well-being. Here's how each of these factors contributes:

1. **Motivational Speeches:**

a. Inspiration and Encouragement: Motivational speeches are aimed at inspiring and motivating listeners to take action, pursue their goals, and overcome difficulties. By focusing on positive affirmations and inspiring themes, motivational speeches can help individuals alter their perspective away from overthinking and self-doubt towards confidence and drive.

b. Perspective Shift: Motivational speeches often offer fresh perspectives and insights into hard situations. They inspire individuals to reframe their beliefs, accept possibilities for progress, and take a more optimistic attitude toward life. This perspective shift can help individuals break free from the cycle of rumination and overthinking, boosting resilience and problem-solving abilities.

c. Emotional Resonance: Effective motivating speeches resonate emotionally with listeners, tapping into their deepest hopes, fears, and wants. By connecting on an emotional level, motivational speakers can inspire people to let go of limiting ideas, confront their fears, and take decisive measures toward personal and professional fulfillment.

d. **Action-Oriented Focus:** Motivational speeches generally emphasize the significance of taking action and moving forward despite hurdles and disappointments. They urge individuals to concentrate their energy and focus on worthwhile tasks rather than being mired down by overthinking and analysis paralysis.

2. **Good Music**:

a. **Mood Enhancement**: Music has the potential to inspire emotions, elevate spirits, and increase mood. Listening to good music can improve mood and lessen feelings of worry and tension, providing a welcome relief from overthinking and negative thought patterns.

b. **Stress Reduction**: Certain forms of music, such as classical, jazz, or instrumental works, have been demonstrated to promote relaxation and reduce physiological markers of stress, such as heart rate and cortisol levels. By establishing a peaceful auditory atmosphere, good music can help folks unwind and quiet their minds, lessening their inclination to overthink.

c. *Mindfulness and Presence:* Music can serve as a tool for mindfulness and presence, helping individuals to be completely involved in the present moment. Immersing oneself in the rhythm and melody of music helps anchor attention, disrupt rumination, and foster a sense of inner serenity and tranquility.

d. **Emotional Expression and Catharsis**: Music provides a medium for emotional expression and catharsis, helping individuals to connect with and process their emotions in healthy ways. Whether through lyrics that relate to personal experiences or instrumental compositions that elicit certain sentiments, good music can facilitate emotional release and bring consolation during times of stress and overthinking.

In summary, motivational speeches and good music can serve as potent antidotes to overthinking by encouraging inspiration, emotional resonance, and stress reduction. By leveraging the transforming power of positive messages and uplifting melodies, individuals may grow resilient, create a more optimistic outlook, and face life's problems with greater clarity and purpose.

GOOD DIET AND MEDITATION

A nutritious diet and meditation can help prevent overthinking and relieve stress through many methods that enhance bodily and mental well-being.

1. **Good Diet**:

a. **Nutrient-rich foods**: Consuming a diet rich in nutrients, including vitamins, minerals, antioxidants, and healthy fats, enhances brain health and cognitive performance. Nutrient-dense foods such as fruits, vegetables, whole grains, lean meats, and healthy fats provide important nutrients that support neurotransmitter synthesis and mood regulation, minimizing the likelihood of stress and overthinking.

b. **constant blood sugar levels**: Eating regular, balanced meals helps maintain constant blood sugar levels throughout the day, reducing energy dips and mood changes. Stable blood sugar levels improve cognitive function and emotional stability, minimizing the chance of stress-induced overthinking and anxiety.

c. Gut-Brain Connection: The gut microbiome has a vital role in regulating mood, stress responses, and cognitive function. A diet rich in fiber and probiotic-rich foods maintains a healthy gut flora, which in turn promotes optimal brain function and mental well-being. By supporting the gut-brain axis, a proper diet can help reduce overthinking and stress-related symptoms.

d. Hydration: Proper hydration is necessary for cognitive function, concentration, and stress management. Drinking a proper amount of water throughout the day helps maintain hydration levels, improves cellular function, and facilitates neurotransmitter production, minimizing the risk of cognitive fatigue and overthinking.

2. Meditation:

a. Awareness practice: meditation cultivates awareness, the practice of being present and nonjudgmental in the moment. Mindfulness meditation practices, such as focused breathing, body scanning, and loving-kindness meditation, assist individuals in gaining awareness of their thoughts and emotions, allowing them to observe and accept them without becoming mired in overthinking or rumination.

b. Stress Reduction: Meditation is a strong strategy for lowering stress and boosting relaxation. By stimulating the body's relaxation response, meditation techniques such as deep breathing and progressive muscle relaxation help drop cortisol levels, decrease heart rate, and generate a mood of quiet and tranquility. Regular meditation practice increases the body's stress response system, making individuals more resilient to stressors and less prone to overthinking.

c. **Emotional Regulation**: Meditation promotes emotional regulation skills, helping individuals to respond to situations with greater equanimity and resilience. By acquiring a higher sense of self-awareness and emotional intelligence, individuals can manage stressful situations more effectively, lessening the tendency to indulge in negative thought patterns and overthinking.

d. **Improved Cognitive Function**: Meditation has been found to enhance cognitive function, including attention, memory, and executive function. By training the mind to focus and sustain attention on the present moment, meditation lowers cognitive distractions and promotes mental clarity, making it easier to break free from overthinking and retain a balanced perspective.

In summary, a nutritious diet and meditation improve stress reduction, emotional well-being, and cognitive resilience, making individuals less sensitive to overthinking and chronic stress. By incorporating healthy dietary habits and mindfulness practices into everyday routines, individuals can develop a supportive environment for mental health and reduce the detrimental impacts of stress and overthinking on general well-being.